Feb 19

Nature-Inspired Innovations

BIO-INSPIRED
TRANSPORTATION AND
COMMUNICATION

Robin Koontz

Rourke
Educational Media

rourkeeducationalmedia.com

Before & After Reading Activities

Building Academic Vocabulary and Background Knowledge

Before reading a book, it is important to tap into what your child or students already know about the topic. This will help them develop their vocabulary, increase their reading comprehension, and make connections across the curriculum.

1. *Look at the cover of the book. What will this book be about?*
2. *What do you already know about the topic?*
3. *Let's study the Table of Contents. What will you learn about in the book's chapters?*
4. *What would you like to learn about this topic? Do you think you might learn about it from this book? Why or why not?*
5. *Use a reading journal to write about your knowledge of this topic. Record what you already know about the topic and what you hope to learn about the topic.*
6. *Read the book.*
7. *In your reading journal, record what you learned about the topic and your response to the book.*
8. *After reading the book complete the activities below.*

Content Area Vocabulary
Read the list. What do these words mean?

aerodynamic
biomimicry
bionic
drag
echolocation
electromagnetic
lobular
pheromones
propulsion
prototypes
sonic boom
tandem
turbulence

After Reading:

Comprehension and Extension Activity

After reading the book, work on the following questions with your child or students in order to check their level of reading comprehension and content mastery.

1. *Why do biomimics study how nature moves and communicates?* (Summarize)
2. *Why does the ability to communicate help animals?* (Infer)
3. *What is an example of improved flight that was inspired by nature?* (Asking Questions)
4. *What transportation and communication skill or skills have you learned from observing nature?* (Text to Self Connection)
5. *What are some animal shapes that help make them move faster?* (Asking Questions)

Extension Activity

Pick an animal that travels in a unique way. What can biomimics copy that would improve a transportation vehicle or system? Draw a design to explain how this new method would improve on the old. Consider things such as energy savings, safety, speed, and reliability.

Table of Contents

Nature-Inspired Travel

An octopus has the ability to whoosh away from predators so fast it seems to disappear. The amazing eight-armed mollusk does it by fleeing head-first. Water goes into the octopus's body, called the mantle. Muscles constrict to close the mantle, squirting water back through a tubular opening called a funnel. The octopus can move the funnel around to steer its hasty retreat.

funnel

mantle

An octopus's amazing flight tricks inspired a new kind of **propulsion** system for watercraft. Researchers built a system using four plastic balls that suck in water and push it back out. The new device is a quiet and fish-friendly alternative to a ship propeller.

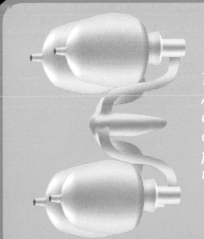

The Octopus Siphon Actuator has four joined elastomer balls, each containing a hydraulic piston. Water is sucked in, then quickly expelled.

Biomimicry, also called biomimetics, involves the study of how functions are delivered in biology, then translating those functions into designs that suit human needs. Architects, scientists, and engineers involved in biomimicry have recognized that nature is the world's largest science and engineering lab.

Over 300 million years of evolution have given dragonflies the ability to quickly fly in six different directions, a feat that biomimicry engineers are very interested in!

Nature has 3.8 billion years of experience! Using nature as inspiration and guide, biomimics research, experiment with, and create innovative designs that help solve human problems. Studying how nature travels and communicates has inspired many new designs in both transportation and communication.

Students in the third Biomimicry Student Design Challenge came up with transportation innovations inspired by nature. One of the winning designs was a human-powered vehicle that mimicked the movements of millipedes and snakes.

bullet train

Birds have given engineers ideas to reduce noise from
air **turbulence** in high-speed trains. Eiji Nakatsu was the

Nakatsu was also inspired by the way a kingfisher dives into the water with barely a splash. He streamlined the nose of the train to look like a kingfisher beak. The new design reduced the **sonic boom** effect the train was causing when it raced out of a tunnel. The new body-style also made the train more energy-efficient.

The odd-looking boxfish is strong and agile with a low body mass. Its design allows the fish to move through the water with little flow resistance.

Engineers copied the body style of a boxfish for a **bionic** car. But the Mercedez-Benz "Bionic" was never marketed. Studies revealed that the boxfish wasn't the best design for power or speed. But it was a good lesson for biomimics.

Mimicking a sailfish had better results. Frank Stephenson of McLaren Automotive knew that sailfish are the fastest fish in the ocean. The designer wanted to know why. He and his team figured out that a sailfish's scales gathered air bubbles that reduced **drag**. This allowed the fish to move faster through the water.

The company lined engine ducts in their P1 hypercar with materials that mimicked the texture of sailfish scales. The change made the car run more efficiently. They also copied aspects of the swordfish's body to make the car more **aerodynamic**.

Natural Flight Innovations

The fastest animal in the air is the peregrine falcon. They can dive 295 feet (90 meters) per second, and yet, it can keep

The designers discovered that the falcon's nostrils are shaped like small protruding cones. They copied the nostril design for the cone in the opening of a jet engine, and resolved the choking issue.

Flying fish are shaped differently from the ribbon halfbeak. Their torpedo-like body lets them speed through the water before they leap into the air and glide for a long distance with their splayed fins.

Flying fish have wing-like fins that get and keep them airborne. There are two wing-like fins in front for "flying," and two wing-like fins in back that provide a steady flight.

Unlike other flying fish, the ribbon halfbeak doesn't have wing-like back fins. To manage flight, they twist their bodies to employ other fins to stabilize them as they soar over the ocean waves. The ribbon halfbeak flying fish is giving designers in Japan new ideas for a certain type of airplane design.

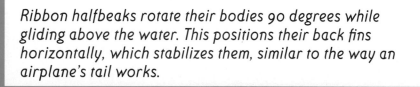

Ribbon halfbeaks rotate their bodies 90 degrees while gliding above the water. This positions their back fins horizontally, which stabilizes them, similar to the way an airplane's tail works.

A tandem wing aircraft has two main wings, one in the front and one to the rear, unlike a biplane with two wings stacked one on top of the other, or a canard design where a small wing is in front and the main wing is in the back.

A **tandem** wing aircraft uses two main wings. One wing is close to the front of the plane and the other is to the rear. The wings work together to give the plane stability and control. The designers are working on an improvement to a tandem wing airplane that mimics the twisting action of the ribbon halfbeak flying fish.

3D printing technology is being used to test new tandem wing airplanes based on the flight of the ribbon halfbeak flying fish. 3D printing is also used in a lot of other biomimicry projects. Being able to create **prototypes** this way gives researchers the freedom to try new ideas more easily.

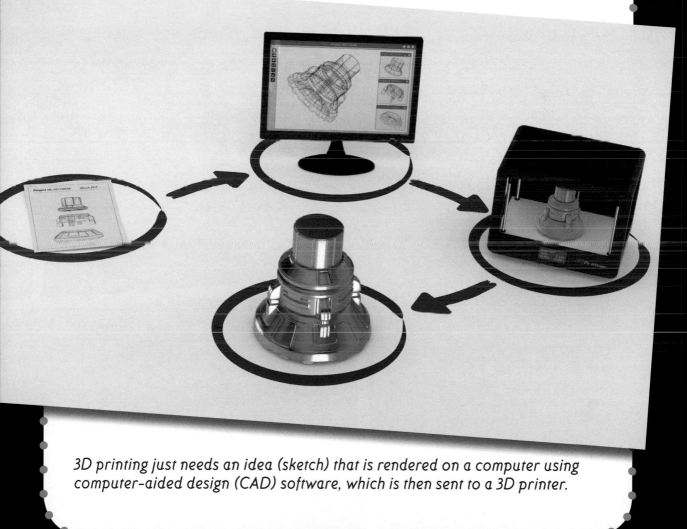

3D printing just needs an idea (sketch) that is rendered on a computer using computer-aided design (CAD) software, which is then sent to a 3D printer.

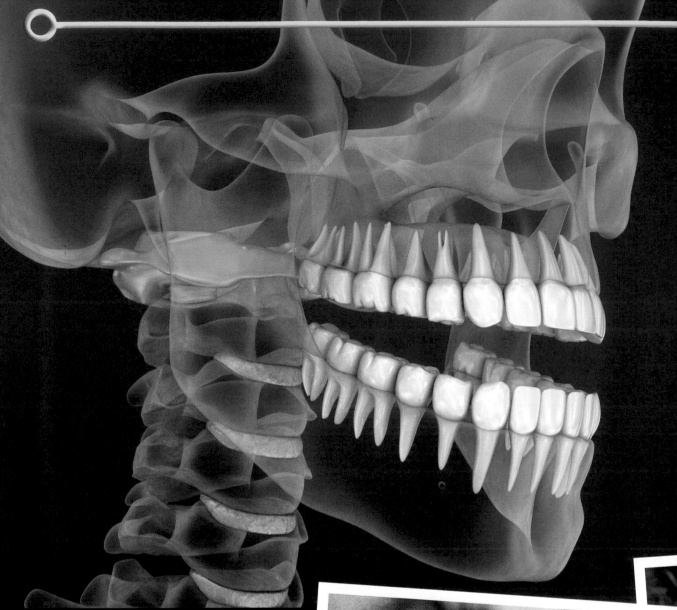

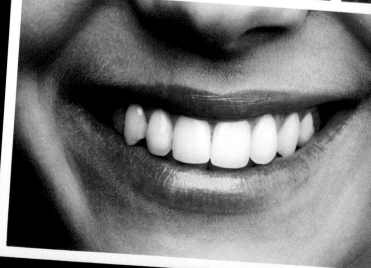

Researchers have been testing human as well as otter teeth to find out how teeth handle stress so well.

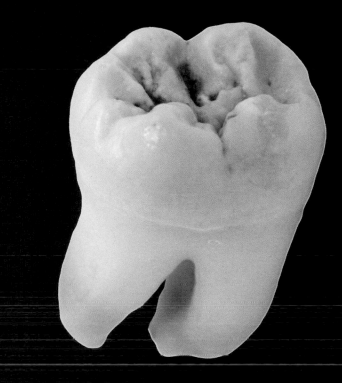

They learned that when damaged, teeth can form a network of tiny cracks instead of one big crack. The smaller cracks can usually heal more quickly, leaving the tooth uninjured.

Attempts to mimic the multi-layered structure of a human or otter tooth could mean a lighter and more crash-resistant material for aircraft.

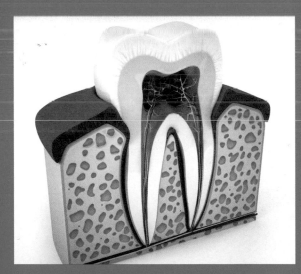

This diagram of a healthy tooth cut in half lengthways shows the layers of the tooth and its internal structure.

Bats are the only mammals that can truly fly. Their amazing flying skills have been mimicked in robotics. But a gliding mammal called a flying squirrel contributed to a fun new innovation for human flight.

Large flaps of skin unfold when a flying squirrel stretches out its arms and legs. The flaps, called patagium, stretch to create a large surface area. The flaps allow the squirrel to lift off and glide between trees or soar gently to the ground.

Designers copied the patagium to create a human wingsuit with large flaps that connect the user's body to the arms. The wingsuits are great fun for skydivers, and something worth considering as a way to get off a cliff in a hurry, and in one piece!

Traffic Control

Ant colonies use swarm intelligence, working together as a social unit, to travel between their colony and a food source. Often called superorganisms, ants and other swarming animals have been an inspiration for more efficient ways to route traffic, both on highways and in the air.

People in the U.S. spend billions of hours a year in traffic jams. Ants never find themselves in that situation. A swarm of army ants will even erect a bridge to keep moving forward.

Researchers discovered that swarms of ants as well as birds, fish, and other swarming animals have simple rules to make travel successful.

Traffic congestion is typical in and around most big cities, making travel difficult and frustrating. Researchers and engineers are always working on ways to improve the steady flow of traffic.

They change direction to allow the main swarm to move without interruption. Using cooperation, they manage to prevent traffic jams. A traffic system based on ant swarms has the potential to increase highway safety, especially with driverless cars.

Problem-solving operations inspired by swarm intelligence are mimicked in other systems as well. Natural gas pipelines, assembly lines, digital storage, and power distribution have all been improved based on how ants and honeybees function in colonies.

A cloud of swarming locusts can contain millions of insects, yet amazingly enough, they almost never collide with one another. Their compound eyes are connected to cells that process electrical and chemical signals in the brain.

Locusts are usually solitary insects, but they also have a swarming phase when millions of them gather and swarm for miles.

Their **lobular** giant movement detector (LGMD) enables the locust to detect anything they might be about to hit. It will quickly adjust its speed or wing movement to avoid a potential accident.

Biomimics discovered that the locust's ability might be applied to automobile safety. Researchers have already mimicked features of the LGMD to develop a computer system that would produce improved collision sensors in cars.

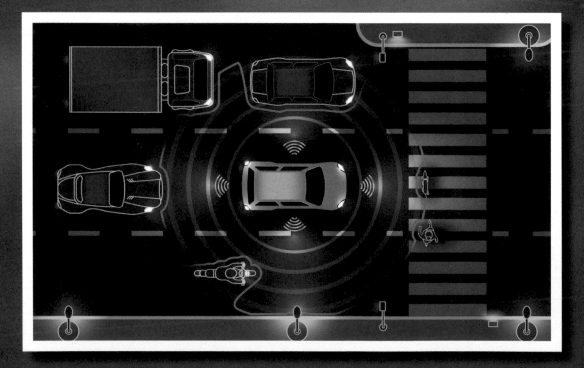

> **"** Biomimicry gives us compelling and hopeful stories for innovation, efficiency, and resilience. It presents a platform of hope and a diverse array of concrete solutions to any challenge. All we need to do is look. **"** – *Tamsin Woolley-Barker, adjunct professor of Biomimicry at Arizona State University*

Locusts are able to fly up to 20.5 miles (33 kilometers) per hour for long distances, and on very limited energy reserves.

Talk Like the Animals

Biomimicry also plays a big part in communication systems. Dolphins are marine mammals that like to feast on fish and squid.

Dolphins make rapid clicking noises that travel underwater and bounce back when the sound waves strike an object. This is called **echolocation**. Dolphins rely on this system to navigate, communicate with others, and avoid predators. They also use echolocation to find a meal.

Sometimes dolphins blow a ring of air bubbles that surrounds a school of fish and traps them. Their sonar can tell them the difference between a bubble and a fish!

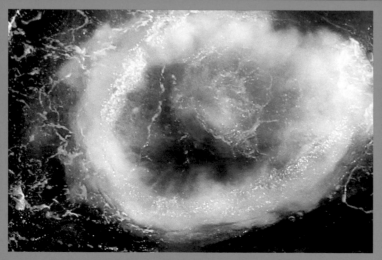

Dolphins expel air when they exhale in the water, creating bubbles, rings, or other formations by controlling the release of their breath and by moving their bodies.

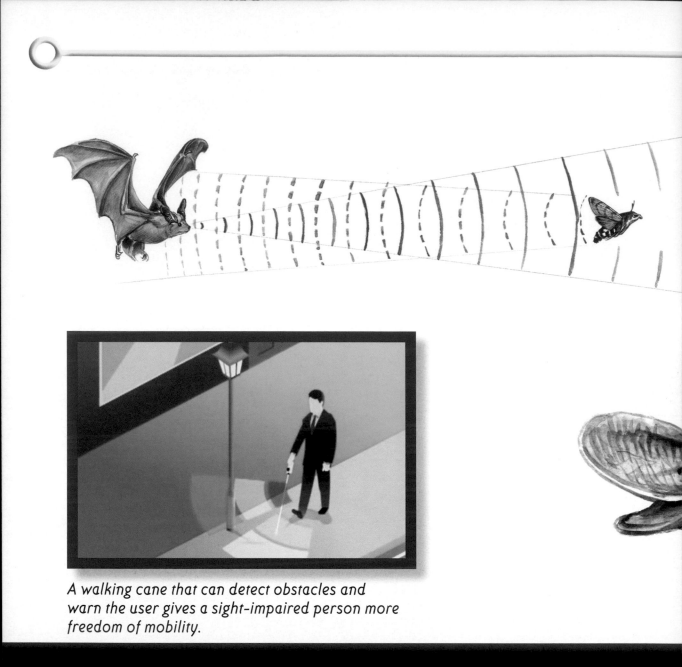

A walking cane that can detect obstacles and warn the user gives a sight-impaired person more freedom of mobility.

Bats also use echolocation to find prey as well as navigate through the night. A bat's amazing sensory system inspired a cane for people who are sight-impaired.

The UltraCane uses a system similar to bat echolocation to detect objects in its path. The cane vibrates when it detects something in the area. The user is able to sense what's going on around them.

Twelve-year-old Alex Deans invented a navigation device for people with visual impairments. Inspired by how bats navigate, Alex created iAid. iAid uses sensors and a joystick to help someone navigate around obstacles without using a cane. Alex hopes to have his bio-inspired product on the market soon.

The handle of an UltraCane has two ultrasound sensors that detect obstacles. The two smaller feedback buttons on the handle vibrate when an obstacle is sensed.

Plants and animals use chemicals to send signals. For instance, bees use chemicals to communicate with other bees. Flowers message bees with their scent in order to entice pollination.

Researchers are studying bio-inspired chemical language. They want to come up with ways to send messages where **electromagnetic** signals won't work, such as in caves, underground pipes, or underwater.

Bees need plants for their pollen and nectar. Flowers benefit because the bees help them to cross-pollinate.

One team successfully created readable chemical messages called molecular communication. Their work prompted more studies for chemical messaging systems in the real world.

Another group of scientists is looking at the way nature communicates for ideas to simplify digital communication. They developed prototypes that mimic the **pheromones** of a female moth.

bombykol molecule

After many years of research, it was the German scientist Adolf Butenandt who discovered the first pheromone, which he and his team called bombykol (BOM-bee-kall), in a female silk moth. Since then, many animals from aphids to elephants have been discovered to also use pheromones to communicate. These chemical messages affect how members of the same species change their behavior.

Saturnia pavoniella

Their tiny device was successful in attracting a male moth. The system has the potential for limitless uses in communication.

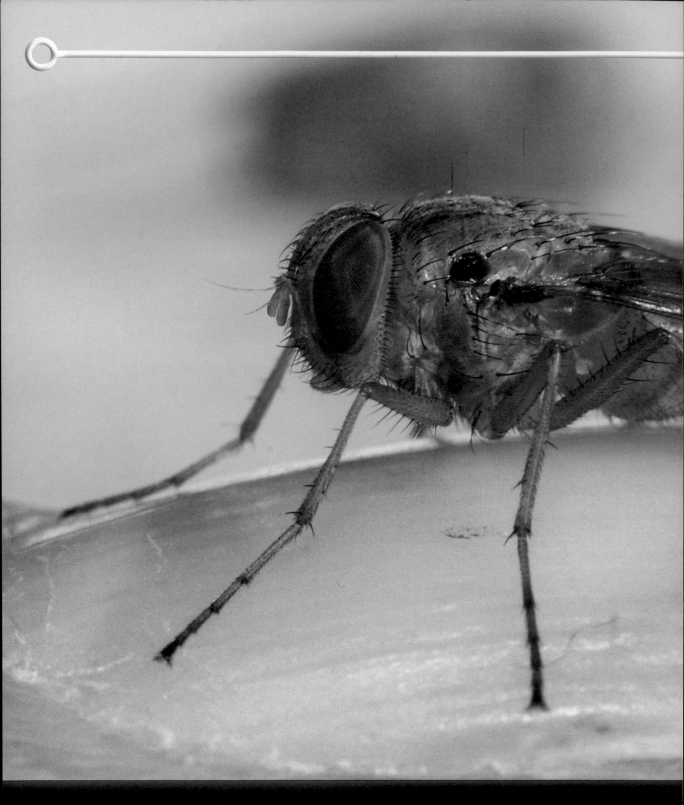

A tiny fly called *Ormia ochracea* has an amazing sense of hearing. Curious researchers found that the two eardrums on the fly are connected with a bendable joint between them.

When one drum reacts to sound, it pushes the other drum. The time difference between the signals tells the fly where the sound is coming from.

Engineers are researching the fly's hearing system to see how they can improve hearing aids and other audio sensors. They've already developed tiny directional microphones in hearing aids.

Nature's time-tested methods for traveling and for communication have inspired scientists to learn new ways that people can move and communicate in more successful and efficient ways.

The Ormia ochracea *female deposits larvae on a male cricket that she located from his song. The larvae soon hatch out and feed on the cricket.*

Glossary

aerodynamic (air-oh-dye-NAM-mik): designed to move through the air easily and quickly

biomimicry (bye-oh-MIM-ik-ree): mimicking nature for solutions to human challenges

bionic (bye-ON-ik): having the ability to perform a physical task increased by special devices

drag (drag): go slowly

echolocation (EK-oh-loh-KAY-shuhn): a process for locating distant or invisible objects by means of sound waves reflected back to the sender from the objects

electromagnetic (i-lek-troe-mag-NET-ik): related to or produced by a magnetism developed by electric current

lobular (lo-byuh-lur): when something looks like a small lobe

pheromones (fer-uh-mones): chemical substances produced and released by an animal for signaling

propulsion (pruh-PUHL-shuhn): the force by which something like a plane or rocket is pushed along

prototypes (PROH-tuh-tipes): the first version of inventions that test to see if they will work

sonic boom (SON-ik boom): the loud noise produced by a vehicle when it travels faster than the speed of sound and breaks through the sound barrier

tandem (TAN-duhm): having two things arranged one in front of the other

turbulence (TUR-byuh-luhnss): not calm or smooth

Index

Show What You Know

1. Why would mimicking a bird beak reduce air noise on a high-speed train?
2. How did sailfish help with car design?
3. How did a peregrine falcon help with airplane design?
4. What ways does echolocation inspire biomimicry?
5. How did flowers give biomimics ideas for new ways to communicate?

Further Reading

Lanier, Wendy Hinote, *Transportation Technology Inspired by Nature*, Focus Readers, 2018.
Koontz, Robin, *Think Like an Engineer*, Rourke Educational Media, 2017.
Vorderman, Carol, *How to Be an Engineer,* DK Children, 2018.

About the Author

Robin Koontz is a freelance author/illustrator of a wide variety of nonfiction and fiction books, educational blogs, and magazine articles for children and young adults. Her 2011 science title, *Leaps and Creeps - How Animals Move to Survive*, was an Animal Behavior Society Outstanding Children's Book Award Finalist. Raised in Maryland and Alabama, Robin now lives with her husband in the Coast Range of western Oregon where she especially enjoys observing the wildlife on her property. You can learn more on her blog: robinkoontz. wordpress.com.

Meet The Author!
www.meetREMauthors.com

© 2019 Rourke Educational Media

www.rourkeeducationalmedia.com

PHOTO CREDITS: Cover: squirrel © Tony Campbell, human ear © Pixsooz, fly © Tawanna08, squirrel suit © Rick Neves; pages 4-5 © Konstantin Novikov; page 6-7 dragonfly © Krasimir Matarov, millipede © PetlinDmitry; page 8-9 train © Vacclav, kingfisher © Butterfly Hunter, kingfisher diving © dreamnikon; page 10-11 boxfish © AnastasiaPetropavlovskaya; page 12-13 car © VanderWolf Images, sailfish © wildestanimal; page 14-15 falcon © Brian Clifford, 2 planes © frank_peters, engine © Lucas Rizzi; page 16-17 photo © Daniel Huebner; page 19 © lucadp; page 20-21 © Billion Photos, tooth illustration © general-fmv, X-ray © Alex Mit, otter © scooperdigital, single tooth © schankz; page 22-23 squirrel © Tony Campbell; page 24-5 main photo © Rick Neves, green wing suit © Aleksei Lazukov; page 26-27 © thatreec; page 28-29 ant bridge © frank60, traffic jam © Alf Ribeiro, page 30-31 © aaabbbccc, inset photo © Vladimir Wrangel; page 32-33 locust © Holger Kirk, illustration © Andrey Suslov; page 34-35 By Willyam Bradberry; page 36-37 © MattiaATH; page 38-39 bats © Panaiotidi, page 40-41 © Mirko Graul, bees and flowers © Happetr, battery illustration © udaix; page 42-43 © Marco Uliana; All photos from Shutterstock.com except: page 10-11 Mercedes "bionic" car © Ryan Somma https://creativecommons.org/licenses/by-sa/2.0/deed.en ; pages 38-39 © www.ultracane.com; page 44-45 fly © https://creativecommons.org/licenses/by-sa/3.0/deed.en

Edited by: Keli Sipperley

Produced by Blue Door Education for Rourke Educational Media. Cover and Interior design by: Nicola Stratford   www.nicolastratford.com

Library of Congress PCN Data
Bio-Inspired Transportation and Communication / Robin Koontz
 (Nature-Inspired Innovations)
 ISBN 978-1-64156-458-8 (hard cover)
 ISBN 978-1-64156-584-4 (soft cover)
 ISBN 978-1-64156-701-5 (e-Book)
Library of Congress Control Number: 2018930691

Rourke Educational Media
Printed in the United States of America, North Mankato, Minnesota